from miss dietz's third-grade class

Advice For a Happy Marriage

debi dietz crawford and friends

WARNER TREASURES

PUBLISHED BY WARNER BOOKS
A TIME WARNER COMPANY

*This book is dedicated
to Debi and Keith*

Warner Treasures is a trademark of

Warner Books, Inc.,
1271 Avenue of the Americas,
New York, NY 10020

Visit our Web site at http://pathfinder.com/twep

A Time Warner Company
Printed in China
First Printing: March 1997
10 9 8 7 6 5 4 3 2 1
ISBN: 0-446-91170-4

Book design by Lisa C. McGarry and Jackie Merri Meyer
Illustrations by Miss Dietz's third-grade class

Contributors
Caitlin, Alana, Shayni, Cori, Britney, Graham, Natania,
Matt K., Lange, Lucy, Tamara, Travis, Chris W., Vanessa, Molly, Michael,
Matt M., Will, Chris A., Shelly, Ashley, Donielle, Eleanor, and Joanie

Message

When I told my third-grade class that I was getting married, I wondered how they would take the news. They were happy, then quickly went back about their business. I didn't think it would make much of an impact—my only worry was how they would handle a week with a substitute teacher when I took my honeymoon.

I needn't have worried. While I was away, my class spent their time scheming with their substitute, Sue Theile, and my partner teacher, Sue Johnson, to create my most cherished wedding gift: ADVICE FOR A HAPPY MARRIAGE. Once they heard Ms. Theile's idea, my students raced to impart all of their advice for our marital future. All of their hopes and dreams of marriage, combined with advice that their eight or nine years of careful observance of their parents' marriages spilled out as fast as their pencils could write.

Soon after our honeymoon, my husband, Keith, appeared in my classroom looking anxious—to my surprise, he had been summoned by my students to help me accept our wedding present. We accepted the gift shyly, under the close scrutiny of twenty pairs of third-grade eyes. Later, when we sat down to enjoy the marital morsel they willed us, we were amazed by the insight offered by the children. Their words were honest, sincere, and startlingly wise. It was their turn to teach *me* something! Today, we treasure our gift, recognizing daily how important it is to continue to see our marriage and our lives through the eyes of a child.

—Debi Dietz Crawford

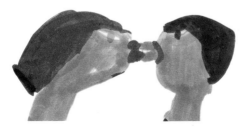

My advice is if there are two cupcakes and the man takes the one with **not** as much frosting, he loves you.

a good

marriage is when

the *man*

lets the

woman

out **first.**

you need to
kiss
every once in
a while.

try to
agree
on things.

love,

never hate.

Share a pet.

if someone comes home **late** from work, don't make a fight about it because they have probably been working too hard.

try not to
get into fights
by trying not to get
angry.

Try to have

triplets.

One child is

too few.

i think you should wear
something beautiful.

have a fun time with celebrations.

make *sure* to celebrate days like halloween.

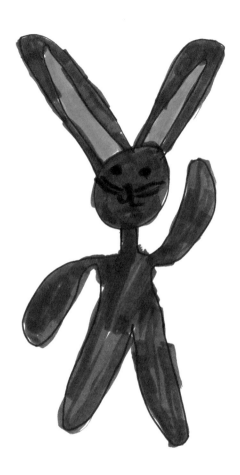

get bunnies.

don't ever get
in fights, it could
cause something

bad to happen.

take turns doing the chores.

When your husband's grumpy,
give him some coffee.

My advice is
to say you **love** each other
for the rest of your lives.

"to show you love
each other, take the
smallest cookie."

i think you should have

2 kids, 4

is too many.

Mostly say

yes.

(Like if you're going
to have hot dogs for
dinner and you really
don't like hot dogs,
it's okay
to say no.)

take
breaks
from
each
other
once
in a
while.

On holidays give presents and love.

give lots of love
to each other
and respect
one another.

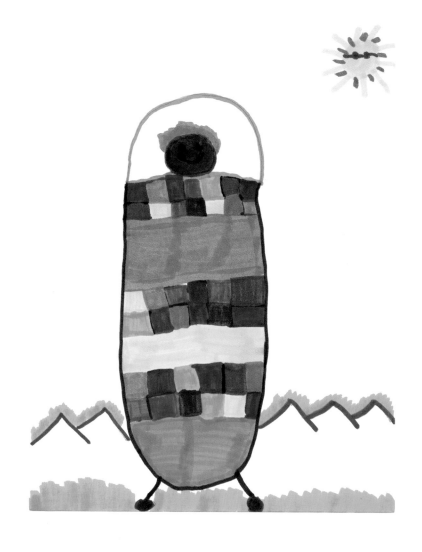

have at least one child.

please
stay
wealthy.

sleep together.

kiss
and make up
when you get into a
fight.

be
together
when
you can.

do
not
marry
another
person.

my advice for a

happy
marriage

is if someone

wants to use some-

thing of the other's, let them use

it. Don't make it

become a fight.

Most important,
have a fun marriage and
love each other
no matter what.